Intrepid Hope
MY PERSONAL JOURNEY TO WHOLENESS

YLAWNDA PEEBLES

GP

GODZCHILD PUBLICATIONS

Published by Godzchild Publications
a division of Godzchild, Inc.
22 Halleck St., Newark, NJ 07104
www.godzchildproductions.net

Printed in the United States of America 2020 - 1st Edition

Library of Congress Cataloging-in-Publications Data
Intrepid Hope: My Personal Journey to Wholeness

ISBN-13 978-1942705949

1. Ylawnda 2. Peebles

2020

This Book is Dedicated to:

My Husband, Joel Robert Peebles, Sr. —
Words are incapable of expressing the love I feel for you.
After 34 years, you continue to light up my life.
You withstand me being your vibrant "Energizer Bunny."
You never complained about me investing over ten hours a day to
writing this book.

My Children — Joel Jr., Jordan, Jeremiah, Janay & Thaddeus
You give me every reason to model the best version of me.
You make the sun shine on a cloudy day.
You are my understanding of *Unconditional Love*.

My Mother, Joyce Ellis Brown —
You consistently represent honor and integrity, at its best.
You taught me everything I know about love and forgiveness.

My Incredibly Beautiful Sisters, Evelyn Denise & Terrie Waynette—
You are examples of grace, kindness and courage.
You are also my best friends, confidants, and prayer partners.

My Church Family, City of Praise Family Ministries —
Indisputably the best spiritual family ever,
you weathered the toughest storm with us and my gratitude runs
deeper than the ocean floor.

My #YPRiseUpGratitudeJourney Gratituders —
God called me to inspire and motivate you,
but you inspire and motivate me.
You are some of the most PHENOMENAL individuals
I've ever had the pleasure of knowing.

TABLE OF
Contents

Foreword

Bishop Joel R. Peebles, Sr., D.D., D.H.L.

Take a deep breath. Now slowly release it. As you slowly exhale, allow the thoughts and feelings of heaviness and daily drudgery to be expelled with every parting breath. At this moment, you are getting ready to embark upon the journey of a lifetime.

As you hold this book in your hands, I sincerely believe that you are prepared to explore the pages that will unlock the freedom which you so desperately desire and deserve.

Each page illuminates the power of HOPE in a world with its fill of brokenness and pain. Yes, it's true, I am a bit biased, as I am the lover and life partner of the author. But before you assume that my heart on this book is built upon a pre-existing relationship, you need look no further than the title to understand the wealth and power within this writing.

Ylawnda uses the most powerful expressions known to man, to bring about enlightenment, healing and freedom. Her extraordinary testimonies and compassionately principled wisdom will not just drive you to tears, but will unearth emotions and truths which lead to health and liberation.

INTREPID HOPE is one of those few books which leaves a lifelong impression upon its reader, allowing them to step out of the mind numbing and emotionally fatiguing experience of daily rigor, in order to find "a better way" to Peace In Christ, Internal Health, Emotional Strength and the undeniable Freedom of Forgiveness.

As you prepare to engage the chapters of this book, I must warn you: there will be areas of your life with unresolved hurts, which have been pricking at you and causing emotional discomfort; but this book will exhume areas of unresolved pain which the enemy placed in your youth, or hurtful moments in your adult life which have caused you grief. All of this will be addressed, and prayerfully, this book will set you on a path of freedom.

It is my strong belief that the words in this writing will speak to your heart, and aid you in your journey to having an unbreakable spirit.

It's time to take the next step on your personal journey to a life of Shatterproof HOPE.

Now, take a breath. Slowly release it and prepare to turn the page. Oh yeah...CONGRATULATIONS IN ADVANCE!

Introduction

Dear Reader,

Beautiful Greetings to you and welcome to my personal journey to wholeness. Grab a nice cup of cold lemonade if you are reading this book during the hot and humid summer months or a cup of warm hot chocolate if there happens to be a frigid chill in the outdoor air. Then locate a private and comfortable place to enjoy each of my authentic testimonies that recount pivotal and sometimes horrific moments in my life I pray they inspires you to embrace the WHOLE and FREE you.

Imagine being an innocent, unblemished and unsuspecting little girl, placed in a world full of complexity and strange norms, both which often lacked empathy. An observer may even believe this world preys on its inhabitants, leaving them broken, wounded and bewildered. The truth is, none of us are exonerated from the stressors of life. The combined tears from each of us could fill all the seas of the earth. The blessing is that each of us, while having experienced deep hurts, has also been given the capacity to learn, mature and conquer every obstacle.

The greatest gift I believe you can gift yourself is that of GROWTH and MATURITY. And the funny thing is that there there is no growth without pain and discomfort and there is no maturity without growth. After growth and maturity, you must pass along your experience to support someone elsein their time of struggle. The inspiration on the pages to come are simplistic. So, e to soar. You are about step on a road which leads to a path, which leads to a course, which leads to a journey which leads you to realizing that the first step you took in CHOOSING to purchase and read this book was enough to make you a champion. Don't be afraid of the bumps in the road. Don't run from the frightening season. Don't get sidetracked by the noisesome pestilence. Remember, you are never alone and the path to wholeness necessitates INTREPID HOPE. Each of us has been granted the power, the anointing and the capacity to overcome anything hurled at us. So, I celebrate what is ahead for you.

From butterflies to eagles, from bondage to freedom, from strangulation to breathing…it's time for you to take flight. The journey begins with one turn of a page and the evolution of the best part of you is about to soar.

LET'S GO!!!!

CHAPTER 1
Move Out of God's Way

Butterflies, in all their captivated beauty and silent signatures of elegance, are what I believe to be God's whisper to creation. They show us, teach us and demonstrate that change is viable. You are not the sum total of the egregious choices you've made, nor the horrific things that have happened to you.

Instead, you are that butterfly; that poetically takes its flight through the air, intentionally avoiding its would-be predator. You are that butterfly that uses its wings to create camouflage patterns to shield yourself from an oncoming attack. You are that butterfly who is nearsighted and can only see a short distance, because you trust The Lord to see what you cannot. You are that butterfly that triumphs its way through the four stages of metamorphosis. You are that butterfly whom God protects and covers during the transformative seasons that can sometimes be violently uncomfortable; yet your victory is inevitable.

YOU ARE THAT BUTTERFLY!
I AM THAT BUTTERFLY!
WE ARE THAT BUTTERFLY!

In 2004, I was pregnant with my youngest son, Jeremiah. In the first trimester of that pregnancy, I was diagnosed with both severe hyperemesis, which is characterized by persistent and severe vomiting that leads to weight loss and possibly life-threatening dehydration, and complete placenta previa, which is when the placenta blocks the opening of the mother's cervix and can result in severe bleeding during pregnancy and delivery. I was bedridden for the entire duration of my pregnancy. The combination of these conditions led to a great deal of complications for us both. When I was slightly over twenty-eight weeks pregnant, I went into labor and the doctors were left with a critical challenge. Delivering the baby via cesarean section or natural birth presented an overwhelming risk of me hemorrhaging to death. The medical team stood frozen with concern and uncertainty, as there was no foreseeable plan of survival for me or my unborn child. After having a plethora of discussions with my husband, they settled on performing a cesarean section. In a little over two hours, our baby was delivered; however, I noticed something unusual. I never heard my baby *cry*. I looked over at my husband, who was seated next to me and delicately caressing my hand, and asked, *"Why isn't my baby crying?"* He responded, "Oh, he's fine. He's fine." But I knew something was dreadfully wrong. I persisted in querying him with, "Why don't I hear him crying? Why isn't my baby crying?!" He repeatedly attempted to reassure me as best he could that our son was fine. However, the moment my husband turned his chair away from me and could no longer look at me, I undoubtedly knew something was heartbreakingly wrong.

The medical staff whisked our baby out of the room. I wasn't even afforded an opportunity to see, hold, or kiss him. Shortly after being sutured from the cesarean section and taken to my private room, we were informed that our baby didn't take a breath for 5 minutes and 4 seconds, and that our baby was brain-dead, on life support and provided nourishment through a feeding tube. They didn't anticipate he would make it through the night. Can you imagine hearing something so earth-shattering, particularly following such a tumultuous pregnancy?

By the Grace of God, Jeremiah made it through the night. The following morning, a team of twelve doctors informed us that he would be a vegetable for the remainder of his life. He would never walk, he would never talk, there would be no quality of life, and we were then advised to participate in home care training.

My trembling flesh desperately desired to embrace fear. The circumstances wanted me to distrust. In those moments, I knew there was nothing I could do to navigate the situation. I felt helpless because I wanted so badly to move and do something. Somewhere in my subconscious, like many of you, I thought God needed my help, but there was nothing I could do except *have faith*. I remember God telling me to move my fear and move my concern out of His Way.

This kind of obedience necessitated humility. It meant humbling myself in order to *move out of God's Way*, and yes, it was paralyzingly difficult. However, difficult does not mean *impossible*. No matter how arduous it is to go through the process of transformation, YOU WILL GET THROUGH IT! YOU WILL OVERCOME! YOU

WILL HAVE A TESTIMONY! From my heart to yours, simply make a CHOICE to *move out of God's Way*.

This season was gut-wrenching and painful. My flesh wanted to dredge up worry. In some cases, the flesh feels comforted in worrying. We can even find ourselves addicted to worrying, evident in pacing the floor, overthinking the problem, losing sleep, or living in the quicksand of denial.

But when I moved, God gave me a vision. In that vision, He said, "If you want to handle this, I will give it to you. Just know, you handcuff Me." In the vision, I not only handcuffed God, but I, too, was handcuffed; handcuffed to my fear, handcuffed to my worry, and handcuffed to thinking I could figure it all out. I was handcuffed into believing that I could plan an escape route. God then said, "If you want Me to handle it, I just need you to move. Move your doubt and let Me handle it. But, if you want to handle it, then *I* will move." I couldn't allow that. I needed my son to live; therefore, I made a CHOICE to give it all to God. I had gone through enough in those six and a half months, and there was no way that I was going to allow it to culminate in the death of my son.

With my simple acquiescence to *move out of God's Way*, I found peace. You, too, will find peace in knowing that you have discarded your cocoon, transitioned through the stages of growth, and your emergence as a "Blossoming Butterfly" was always closer than you thought. Think back to when you were a child and you needed help. You may have called on your mother or father, grandmother or grandfather. You called on whomever you believed had the authority and power to resolve the problem. God is our Father, and He has the Power to make everything beautiful in its time.

"He hath made everything beautiful in his time…"
Ecclesiastes 3:11

My husband and I would stay in the Neonatal Intensive Care Unit (NICU) nearly seventeen hours a day, praying and confessing God's Word over our son. Not once did we entertain a conversation regarding the devastating report. We, instead, continued to confess God's Word over him. We would declare the truth from scriptures like *Romans 8:16-17;* Our son was somebody, *"a child of God, and a co-heir with Christ,"* and *Isaiah 53:4-5; "Surely, He has borne our griefs and carried our sorrows; yet we esteemed Him stricken, smitten by God, and afflicted. But He was wounded for our transgressions, He was bruised for our iniquities; the chastisement for our peace was upon Him, and by His stripes, our son was healed."* We stood on those TRUTHS. Scripture after scripture after scripture, we refused to give up, and miraculously, on the third day, *a Sunday at that*, God turned things around.

That Sunday, my husband, who never left my side, told me that he wasn't going to go preach that morning. He desired to go with me down the hall, as we did every day, to sit and pray over our son. I gazed at him and expressed to him why he couldn't make that decision. "You should go and teach so God can save the lives of the people that He ordained to be saved on this day. I'll stay here and continue prayer over our baby. Don't worry about us, we'll be fine." When he left, still in unrelenting pain from the surgery and in my hospital wheelchair, I rolled myself all the way down to the NICU. When I arrived, one of the doctors stopped me and said, "Mrs. Peebles, we have a surprise for you!" I was overwhelmed with elation to hear some good news. When she told me to look at the baby, I was perplexed. He was still in an incubator with tubes covering his tiny and frail body. No matter how hard I tried, I couldn't visibly see a difference. She said, "Mrs. Peebles, your baby is off of life support." My baby, my Jeremiah, was now off of life support! I was so grateful to God; I fell to the ground a few times. God took our son off of life support on the third day, a Sunday. I immediately called my husband and he instantaneously responded, "I'm on my way!" I advised him to continue on his journey to church, but he wouldn't have it any other way, and made his way back to the hospital.

I will forever remember the woman who presented us with the news. She was short in stature, but her personality was as big as her heart. She said to us, "I don't know what it is about you and your husband, but there's something very special about the two of you, and God sent me to pray for your child." This was the lead NICU doctor, and she then called her staff over to the center of the NICU and gave them detailed instructions. "I want you all to care for every one of these babies." Then she gestured toward our son, "But this baby better live, and if there's nothing else, I'm going to go pray for him." We stood in astonishment and awe, to say the least.

Once the doctor made her exit to pray, we sat close to the incubator that encased our son, continuing to confess God's Word over him. Then, God showed me another vision. It was so clear, it was as if I could touch it. I saw a vision of God's Hand gently placed on our son's chest. After I saw that vision, I said to God, "I've heard the report; but Lord, I'm trusting in You. I trust that I'll be able to take him home any way You give him to me. I know everything they said, but Lord, I'm putting You in remembrance of Your Word that we will have the desires of our hearts, and our desire is that you make Jeremiah whole: spirit, soul, and body.

"Delight Thyself also in the Lord and He shall give thee the desires of thine heart." Psalm 37:4

God heard and answered our prayers, just as He will hear and answer your prayers, according to *I John 5:15*, *"And if we know that he hears us, whatever we ask, we know that we have what we asked of him."*

Jeremiah would be in the NICU until the seventh day, which was completely inconceivable considering the reports we received. We were also told that our son tested positive for Down's Syndrome, and we prepared to undergo all the necessary training to endlessly care for him. Yet, on the seventh day, the doctor gave us a new report! A different doctor came in and told us that Jeremiah would be discharged that afternoon, and we could take our baby home! What's interesting is that we never saw the lead NICU doctor again, and we believe in our hearts that she was an angel.

"Be not forgetful to entertain strangers: for thereby some have entertained angels unaware." Hebrews 13:2

At the time of the writing of this book, Jeremiah is sixteen years old. He has had TOTAL VICTORY over EVERY report given by the doctors. He attended Georgetown University at the age of fifteen with a 4.0

GPA. I neglected to inform you that the doctors had also originally told us that Jeremiah did not pass his hearing or vision test. Glory to God in the Highest, that, too, was not his testimony.

Our family is a studious one, and we value education. My husband and I have two doctorates each, our eldest son is in law school, our daughter, middle son, and soon to be son-in-love, are all in their master's programs; but, with all of the degrees in our home, God granted our youngest son an extra dose of brilliance and intellect.

We always keep these scriptures close to our hearts, particularly during our darkest hours, and I pray it motivates you to do the same.

"And the glory of your latter house will be greater than the former and, in this place, you will have peace." Haggai 2:9

"To appoint unto them that mourn in Zion, to give unto them beauty for ashes, the oil of joy for mourning, the garment of praise for the spirit of heaviness; that they might be called trees of righteousness, the planting of the Lord, that he might be glorified." Isaiah 61:3

I pray my testimony encourages you. God is Real. God is Alive and God knows precisely what you need.

"Be not ye therefore like unto them: for your Father knoweth what things ye have need of, before ye ask him." Matthew 6:8

The words in the Bible are true. I know because I've experienced the Love of God for myself. I have read His Letters of Love written to me and to you in His Word.

I've seen the manifestation of His Work. Every time I look at our son and reflect on how he began reading Plato and Kierkegaard at the age of eight, it's a sobering reminder of just how Real our God Is. He's Real and He wants to step into your situation. He wants you to live and enjoy a FREE LIFE!

"…I am come that they might have life, and that they might have it more abundantly." John 10:10

IT'S YOUR TIME TO FLY BUTTERFLY…FLY!!!

FOCUS SCRIPTURE:

"Trust in the LORD with all your heart and lean not on your own understanding; in all your ways submit to him, and he will make your paths straight." Proverbs 3:4-6

"No one will be able to stand against you all the days of your life. As I was with Moses, so I will be with you; I will never leave you nor forsake you." Joshua 1:5

CALL TO ACTION:

Breathe and take a moment to reflect. What areas in your life are in God's way? Is it fear? Self-doubt? Unforgiveness? If you are unsure of where those areas are, ask God to illuminate them for you. I want you to really dig deep and write those areas down. Make a choice to stand down and trust God to move and annihilate those things in your life. God will not move in an area unless we move out of it. Make the choice to do things differently.

CHAPTER 2
Get Off the Ferris Wheel

The outdoor air is fragranced with the scent of deep-fried funnel cakes and caramel glazed popcorn. The melodious sounds of laughter and playful screams are vaguely heard in the distance. The scenic drive through the mysterious but photographic safari harmonizes with the calming and reverberating echoes from the water park rides. The intrepid joy of the long-awaited roller-coaster ride is upon us; and who could neglect the sedentary thrills of the infamous FERRIS WHEEL?

The Ferris Wheel is a metaphor for the basic pattern of human experiences. Unlike with other amusement park rides, Ferris Wheel riders refrain from the quintessential audible screams of elation because they feel more comfortable and secure with the leisurely pace. It is notorious for going in circles, and it is exempt of a destination.

The Ferris Wheel boldly resembles the functionality of life, consistently reminding us not to live life at full speed, but to pause and live in the moment. Be cognizant and enjoy the sounds of birds singing as you rise in the morning and hear the chorus of crickets humming in the night. Like Ferris Wheels, we experience highs and lows in life; however, if we remain calm, steadfast and appreciate the lessons to be learned, God will always bring us back to the top.

"Fear thou not; for I am with thee: be not dismayed; for I am thy God: I will strengthen thee; yea, I will help thee; yea, I will uphold thee with the right hand of my righteousness."
Isaiah 41:10

Although the Ferris Wheel can take you on an enjoyable ride, very relaxed, with numerous journeys, there are times when you have to be valiant. At times, you must make a CHOICE to get off of the Ferris Wheel. Abandon those issues, circumstances and people that have taken you in circles, resulting in the same outcome of hurt, anger, brokenness, low self-esteem and unforgiveness. Isn't that customary of the enemy, who uniquely makes you feel exceptionally comfortable with going in circles, but headed nowhere?

Can you ruminate on a period of time when you felt like you were moving but simultaneously going nowhere? Have you ever been exhausted and weary with being exhausted and weary, but nothing changed? If that resembles your life, you are not alone, and I pray this testimony aids you in getting off your Ferris Wheel, as I too had to do.

When I was a young child, my father died suddenly and unexpectedly. In the shadow of his passing, my mother learned that she was pregnant with my younger sister, but my father was unaware that my mother was pregnant at the time of his passing. My mother, my queen and my shero, was my first example of a woman of faith, and it was that unflinching nature that maintained her strength when she was abruptly left to raise two children and another that would soon make her entrance into the world.

My mother never wavered in her love for God, nor her steadfastness in raising her daughters, whom she affectionately called her "Three Bees"; Bumble-Bee, my eldest and beautiful sister Evelyn Denise, Honey-Bee, myself, and Bee-Bee, my youngest and lovely sister Terrie Waynette. Mother has always walked as a wise woman, showering us with the appropriate doses of love and discipline. She has always modeled for us, what a phenomenal woman is — in word, in conversation and in deed. Thanks to the best mother in all the land, Queen Joyce Ellis Brown.

My father's death stung us all to the Mariana Trench of our souls. His death was the beginning of a cruel cycle for me. I also experienced the murder of my most beloved aunt, after which, the death of my uncle, followed by the death of my mother's best friend; shortly after that, the deaths of my grandmother and grandfather. My life was being shaped by death. The enemy was aware of this, and used it to weaponize and define my perception of the world. Throughout my life, he was growing this suffocating vine of fear that wrapped itself around me daily, and kept me cycling on what seemed like a never-ending Ferris Wheel.

I was blind to how the enemy was strategically creating a pathology of fear and worry. The enemy wanted to define my life's canvas. Fear presented itself in the way I responded to things and how I navigated my life. It was attached to my decisions and emotions. It was happening every day, and it was attempting to kill me. I didn't realize I was trapped on a Ferris Wheel that enslaved me to fear, and I wouldn't learn the truth until I had my children, namely my daughter Janay.

My daughter is the perfect image of me. She responds like me, talks like me, smiles like me, and often thinks like me. We say, "Oh that's precious" to the same things. We're crestfallen about the same things and overjoyed about the same things. It wasn't until I realized how much of myself I saw in her, that I also realized there was an enormous conundrum. The fear that was living in me was also living in her, and it was my responsibility to annihilate that generational curse.

As a result of countless attacks from bullies in school and the deaths of my husband's family, fear was becoming a crippling experience for my daughter, which mirrored my life. As an honor student, choir singer, lead actress in school plays, member of the chess club and a member of the dance company, she began to eat lunch in the restroom to conceal herself from the bullies. Consequently, my husband and I made an expeditious decision to have our daughter see a counselor. During counseling, while my daughter was speaking, I had the most dreamlike epiphany. As I compassionately gazed at her, I no longer saw her; but was looking at the little girl in me that never dealt with the FERRIS WHEEL OF FEAR and how it was suffocating me. At which point, I knew I had to do the hard work to be free from this Ferris Wheel.

Perhaps you find yourself on this same or similar Ferris Wheel and you desperately wish to end the ride and make a better CHOICE for your life. Well, YOU ARE NOT ALONE! I had to make the same CHOICE to participate in my own freedom. I went to God in prayer, knowing I couldn't delay it until tomorrow, next week, or even the next month. I told God, "Freedom has to take place today, and with Your Help, God, I can become more than a conqueror."

"Nay, in all these things we are more than conquerors through him that loved us." Romans 8:37

God responded,

"Fear thou not, for I am with thee: be not dismayed; for I am thy God: I will strengthen thee; yea, I will help thee: yea I will uphold thee with the right hand of my righteousness." Isaiah 41:10

Weeks and months tiptoed by while I was working to conquer the fear in every way I knew how. It began to feel like the more I worked to face it, the worse it became. During a routine wellness visit to my family practitioner, I explained what I was undergoing regarding the debilitating effects of fear. I was fearful of driving, swimming, flying and traveling. She responded, "Don't worry, Dr. Peebles, we can put you on some medication to assist with that." I asked God, "Where are You? Where is my solution? Help me overcome this." God's response was, "Daughter, why are you waiting for Me, when I'm waiting for *you?*" God was waiting for me to make a CHOICE to get off of the Ferris Wheel, this never-ending cycle that repeated itself over and over and over again, but ultimately resulted in nothing.

Leaving the doctor's office, I knew I wanted to conquer this with God and not medication. That day,

I began a journey to defeat every fear that had me on a vicious cycle. For some, medication is a practical solution. For others, it may necessitate counseling, and for a few, it may be necessary to have both medication and counseling. I support you on the path that works best for you. I smile as I type, because God has brought me so far, and soon, you will experience the same.

I trusted God and did the assiduous work to defeat every single fear. I promised God that once I jumped off the *Ferris Wheel of Fear*, I would never return to that turbulent ride again. I then reminded myself of this verse in Scripture, *"As a dog returns to its vomit, so a fool repeats his folly" Proverbs 26:11.* When you CHOOSE to give your fears to God, the enemy will work more diligently to entice you to get back on the Ferris Wheel, but just remember,

> *"The name of the Lord is a strong tower: the righteous runneth into it, and they are safe." Proverbs 18:10*

Subsequently, you have the authority!

> *"I have given you authority to trample on snakes and scorpions and to overcome all the power of the enemy: nothing will harm you." Luke 10:19*

Now that you know you have the authority, I leave with you seven pivotal keys to aid you in Getting Off Your Ferris Wheel.

1. Pray
2. Make a CHOICE
3. Face Your Fears

4. Rid Yourself of All Regret
5. Appreciate Living in the Moment
6. Create a Strong Support System
7. Visualize Being FREE

"Commit to the Lord whatever you do, and your plans will succeed." Proverbs 16:3

God is with you and has never left you; but, you have a responsibility in your process and journey to FREEDOM.

"This book of the law shall not depart out of thy mouth; but thou shalt meditate therein day and night, that thou mayest observe to do according to all that is written therein: for then thou shalt make thy way prosperous, and then thou shalt have good success." Joshua 1:8

You don't know who you really are until you know the FREE you. Make a CHOICE today, to fight for your FREEDOM. Accept your past, process the pain; then give it to God and live your life!

FOCUS SCRIPTURE:

"Therefore, if any man be in Christ, he is a new creature: old things are passed away; behold, all things are become new."
II Corinthians 5:17

CALL TO ACTION:

Identify the cycles in your life that keep you circling on the Ferris Wheel. Write down what they are and determine what is needed to get off and remain off.

CHAPTER 3
Live Life to Its Fullest

Have you ever noticed the different shades of blue that majestically paint the sky? Have you ever noticed the air, ripe with petrichor after it rains? Have you ever observed the leaves of a tree dancing in the wind? Have you ever stopped to enjoy the feeling of sun rays resting on the surface of your skin?

As testified in the previous chapter, I was sinking in a "Tsunami of Fear," which prevented me from living a free life. It also distorted the lens by which I viewed my life. I was void of seeing the beautiful tapestry of colors God placed in this world. Instead, I was left seeing the gray, overcast clouds of anguish that obstructed the sunshine. When fear robs you of your quality of life, you are not living; you are simply existing. Everyday seems gloomy. You miss the flowers blooming. You become unresponsive to the sounds of happiness. The fear engrosses you and extracts everything from you like a leech. Every day is like being a lamb headed to slaughter.

As with many of you, fear caused me to consistently be in pursuit of a safety net. I found myself always strategizing on what needed to be done to feel comfortable wherever I was going. My thoughts were consistently highjacked with developing plans to help navigate my life around the fear. I often cried tears of despair, thinking this would forever be a part of me. But one beautiful sunny afternoon, following a conversation with my incredible and handsome husband, I decided to make a life-altering CHOICE.

I was having an issue with my breast, to which my husband advised me to schedule an appointment to get a breast sonogram and mammogram. This became a recurring appointment every three months for an entire year. During one of the visits, the doctor told me my results were unusual and I needed to see a breast surgeon to rule out breast cancer. The diagnosis came at a very tumultuous time in our lives. We were grieving the passing of my husband's mother and having major issues with six employees of our church attempting a hostile takeover, and I remember saying, "Dear God, how much shall we be made to endure?"

The added weight of the health concern felt like yet another daunting hole in our souls during this unrelenting storm. I remember crying out to The Lord, "I am a woman of faith who can cast her cares on you; but I need you, Lord, to help the parts of me that don't believe."

"Jesus said to him, if you can believe, all things are possible to him who believes. Immediately the father of the child cried out and said with tears, Lord, I believe; help my unbelief!"
Mark 9:23-24

Following that prayer, I passionately expressed to my husband, "Please agree with me in prayer and trust God with me. Together, we must prove the devil is still a liar."

OKAY, ONE SECOND. I HAVE TO STOP AND GIVE HIM SOME PRAISE FOR ALL OF THE GOOD THINGS HE HAS DONE. SHOUTING GLORY... HALLELUJAH... THANK YOU JESUS... YOU NEVER FAIL, IN THIS VERY MOMENT!

Okay, I'm back.

I thought my husband was going to give me a superfluous soliloquy of Biblical words and scriptures. I was surely waiting for it. Instead, he patiently and lovingly took me by the hand, looked me in my eye, and called me by his special nickname for me. "Red Silk, listen to me, JUST LIVE." I said, "Yes, Sir!" To which he replied, "You don't hear me!" This time I said, "Yes, Sir! I got it...JUST LIVE!" He repeats, "You don't hear me!" We went back and forth a few more times because I thought I understood what he meant and he was adamant that I didn't. Ultimately, he exclaims, "No, you don't hear me. I don't care what the report says nor what's happening with the church. I know it's scary; but I am telling you to JUST LIVE! Live in the moment, JUST LIVE! Red Silk, smile, laugh, go outside, JUST LIVE! That's the plan. I want you to promise me you will JUST LIVE!"

Beloved, do not let pain nor fear keep you from living your life. Take a deep breath and know that God is still with you. Read God's Word and remember that He has never left you. Go outside and yell audibly, "God is Good," if that's what it takes. Scream into your pillow; shout Glory to God. Dance in the rain. Have dinner with your siblings. Enjoy lunch with friends. Start a bonfire. Roast marshmallows. Watch a movie called *The Notebook*. Take notes to Bishop Joel Peebles' Sunday Sermons.

No matter what people say about you. No matter what the doctor's report reads. No matter how many people reject you. No matter the lies told on you. No matter how many times you've failed. No matter how many times you've started over.

NO MATTER WHAT...JUST LIVE!

As long as God grants me time on this side of heaven, I will continuously remind myself to "JUST LIVE!" And my prayer for you is that you do the same. Congratulations on CHOOSING to JUST LIVE! Your life will never ever, never ever, be the same again.

FOCUS SCRIPTURE:

"O Lord by these thing men live, and in all these things is the life of my spirit: so wilt thou recover me, and make me to live." Isaiah 38:16

Examine and identify the ways that you are going to choose to live. Are you going to get up thirty minutes earlier to meditate? Are you going to schedule some time to go for walks and enjoy the outdoors? Make a choice to live!

CHAPTER 4
Make Unconditional Love Your First Choice

The Greatest Wonder of the World; it's the aroma that accents the crisp noonday air. It's God's strikingly crafted autograph of INTREPID HOPE. It's the culmination of honesty and commitment. It miraculously surrenders to our free will. It outlasts the most catastrophic storm and takes us on an intimate journey of undeniable triumph.

That Greatest Wonder of the World is UNCONDITIONAL LOVE. It is *selfless*. It is *infinite*. It is *altruistic*. It is *limitless*. It is *authentic*. However, there are times when extending unconditional love can be laborious and heavy on the heart.

My husband's mother, Apostle Betty Poindexter-Peebles, was admired by most for being the first female pastor of a mega church, co-founded with her husband, Bishop James R. Peebles, Sr., Jericho Baptist Church, later Jericho City of Praise (currently City of Praise Family Ministries). While enduring the grief of burying her husband (Bishop James R. Peebles Sr.) and her two eldest sons (Pastor James R. Peebles Jr., and Pastor John R. Peebles Sr.), Apostle Betty, whom I affectionately called, "Momma Dutch," had fallen terminally ill to her second bout with colon cancer and was fighting for her life. She was unable to lead the church as she had done flawlessly for over forty years, when six of her employees secretly conspired a hostile takeover. During that time, the church was in the intermediate stages of multiple projects. While these projects were going on, the enemy came in to steal, to kill, and to destroy.

"The thief cometh not, but for to steal, and to kill, and to destroy: I am come that they might have life, and that they might have it more abundantly." John 10:10

On October 12, 2010, seven days after her seventy-sixth birthday, Apostle Betty closed her eyes for the final time on earth. Just three days later, the six employees slammed my husband and another board member, William A. Meadows, with a temporary restraining order, banning them from being on the church campus. They were ordered to appear in court the following morning at eight o'clock. If unprepared with a defense, the order would be in effect and my husband would not have been permitted to attend his mother's homegoing service at the church. BUT, to our God be all the Glory, the judge denied their order and ruled in our favor.

"Yet when they cried out to the Lord in their trouble, the Lord brought them out of their distress. He calmed the storm and its waves quieted down. So they rejoiced that the waves became quiet, and he led them to their desired haven." Psalm 107:28–31

Bishop Joel Peebles, Sr., & Chairman William A. Meadows

God truly is in control and He uses people to get His breakthrough and blessing to you.

"And I will bless those who bless you, and the one who curses you I will curse. And in you all the families of the earth will be blessed." Genesis 12:3

Therefore, with a sincere heart of gratitude and a standing ovation, I salute our outstanding General Council, Bobby G. Henry Jr., his wife, Debra Palmer-Henry and Roderick Chavez, for their importunity and dedication in presenting the truth in this case. And I ask God daily, to bless them and their families in ways that exceed their expectations.

STANDBY, I NEED ANOTHER PRAISE BREAK! GOD IS BETTER THAN GOOD!

Okay, I'm back!

Following Momma Dutch's Homegoing Service, my husband requested a meeting with the six employees. He discovered that members of the original Board of Directors (who served for 20-40 years), were illegally removed and the employees asserted themselves as the active Board of Directors. Their claim was that my husband was never a member of the Board. These employees also sought to micromanage and control my husband, who at that time had served as the Assistant Pastor for thirteen years, in an effort to control the financial, administrative and spiritual decisions. Our salaries were dissolved, our health insurance was discontinued, and every Friday a process server delivered an acrimonious letter to our home. We were betrayed by the media, community leaders, spiritual leaders and lawyers, to name a few. That "Twilight Zone" nightmare was the equivalent of a turbulent aircraft just taking flight, with no certainty of what was ahead.

Bewildered, but enjoying a beautiful Wednesday sunrise and clear blue skies, we headed to the church campus for a full day of meetings, unaware of the tornado our lives were soon to face. While we were in my husband's office, a loud knock shifted the main door. Before we could rise to open it, a letter was shoved underneath. All I can remember is the letter asking us to indefinitely leave the premises. The campus was surrounded by state and local police, who were hired to escort us off of our beloved campus. We were paraded around and treated like criminals. The amount of force was excessive. One officer even shoved my husband into the wall. It was absolute chaos. In all their attempts to provoke us to respond aggressively, they realized we were maintaining our God-like composure and decided to escort us out of the building almost two hours after their arrival.

This church was our entire life. Teaching, aiding, counseling, and providing services of hope were all we knew. I had served in the ministry since I was fifteen years old, and my husband was born into ministry. His parents

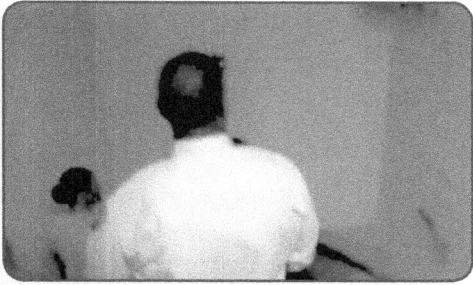

founded the ministry five years prior to his birth. The copious amount of pain we both felt was indescribable. News of what was taking place had spread like wildfire and there was already an overwhelming mob of people, journalists and television reporters waiting for us to emerge from the administration building. It was one of the most devastating days in both of our lives. I was frightened. I felt broken. I wallowed in confusion. Even today, it's difficult to accept that this was an experience that happened in our lives. My heart and soul wailed in anguish and I couldn't believe this was happening. We had invested our lives loving and caring for people. I was dumbfounded and left wondering, *"How did we get here?"* However, as we were chaperoned down the stairs toward the front of the administration building, I heard the Lord say, "You love your crystal, right?" I was perplexed. "What do you mean, God?" He said, "You protect your crystal, right? You keep your crystal in a safe place because it's fragile and valuable. I want you to protect your husband and the vision I've given him, in the same manner." He continued, "So you don't have the luxury of being angry or hurt, disappointed or sad. Right now, your job is to stand strong, side by side with your husband and Trust My Process, no matter how difficult is becomes." And my journey began in a way I could never have imagined.

I vacillated with the best way to withstand this trial, and my answer was not far away. UNCONDITIONAL LOVE. That standard of Love would be our breath when we felt alone. That standard of Love would be our keeping power when we lost court cases. That standard of Love kept our minds sound when we sat confused. I remember telling myself that love has to win or there is no God, and I knew that wasn't the case. I reminded myself that God knew about the battle before we did, and our outcome was predicted.

"Owe no man anything but to love one another: for he that loveth another hath fulfilled the law." Romans 13:8

I decided to CHOOSE LOVE to guide my path. It wasn't easy because I wanted to hide in a corner and just cry. I needed to understand what the impact would be on my children, our church family, and the non-believers who read or heard about this bickering within the church. I was vexed that the non-believers would never turn to God because this was happening among people who claimed to love and serve God. So many thoughts swirled around in my head and heart. I felt broken and embarrassed. We didn't do anything wrong, but we knew that people were going to perceive what they wanted, based on what they thought was factual. My heart broke for my husband because he was still mourning the death of his mother, in fact, the death of his entire core family. How could a Loving God allow such a thing to take place?

As you reflect on something traumatic that took place in your life, you may be in a space where you are asking that exact same question. Be encouraged that the storms won't last always and God will make everything beautiful in its time.

"He hath made everything beautiful in his time: also, he hath set the world in their heart, so that no man can find out the work that God maketh from the beginning to the end."
Ecclesiastes 3:11

I didn't know how God was going to work it out, but I knew He was going to work it out, because I had *present* confidence based on my *past* experience with Him. I followed God's Love Plan, and forty months to the day that we were wrongfully excommunicated from the church, the court ruled in our favor again and sent us back to our spiritual home. With all things stacked against us, it was nothing else but God, and if He did it for us, He will surely do it for you.

"Jesus Christ the same yesterday, and today, and forever."
Hebrews 13:8

When you stand on God's Promises and CHOOSE UNCONDITIONAL LOVE, you also CHOOSE VICTORY. I can't promise you how God will do it, nor when; however, rest in the truth that it is already done and your unconditional love is what manifests it.

"There hath no temptation taken you but such as is common to man: but God is faithful, who will not suffer you to be tempted above that ye are able; but will with the temptation also make a way to escape, that ye may be able to bear it."
I Corinthians 10:13

As a bonus, I wanted to share three scriptures that, I pray, will catapult you in your ability to LOVE. Hold them near and dear. Walk them out and wait patiently for God to reveal the breakthrough.

"God is not a man, that he should lie; neither the son of man, that he should repent: hath he said, and shall he not do it? Or hath he spoken, and shall he not make it good?"
Numbers 23:19

Perfect Love casts out fear.

"There is no fear in love; but perfect love casteth out fear: because fear hath torment. He that feareth is not made perfect in love." I John 4:18

Perfect Love is God.

"Beloved, let us love one another: for love is God: and everyone that loveth is born of God, and knoweth God. He that loveth not knoweth not God; for God is Love."
I John 4:7-8

There is no better time than the present to pause and reflect on the times when God's Love brought you through tumultuous times.

Now then, give Him Thanks.

"I will praise thee, O Lord, with my whole heart: I will shew forth all thy marvelous works." Psalm 9:1

FOCUS SCRIPTURE:

"Love is patient and kind; love does not envy or boast; it is not arrogant or rude. It does not insist on its own way; it is not irritable or resentful; it does not rejoice at wrongdoing, but rejoices with the truth. Love bears all things, believes all things, hopes all things, endures all things. Love never ends."
I Corinthians 13:4-8

CALL TO ACTION:

Write down the names of those who hurt you. Then write down the ways that you can show them love. Examples: *Pray for them. Give them an encouraging word. Write a kind letter or send flowers.*

CHAPTER 5
Embrace Your Self Worth

I t's the strong and welcomed presence of a father when life seems bitter and challenging. It's a mother's gentle embrace while she offers much needed advice. It's the laughter with a long-time friend, following a demanding day. It's the imperfect reflection in the mirror; yet you still settle in contentment. Understanding your worth is the foundation of weathering a storm. Knowing Who and Whose you are, reassures you when victory seems unobtainable. You are worthy of love! You are worthy of respect! You are worthy of God's best. Never ever falter to any other opinion!

Perhaps there have been seasons when you felt unworthy of love, friendship, or success, so I pray you find courage in my testimony and make a commitment to stand tall, walk gracefully and trust the INTREPID strength and audaciousness that you have always possessed.

Embracing your self-worth immobilizes your enemy and allows you to walk in the liberty wherein Christ has set you free. Once free, make a personal commitment to never be entangled with unworthiness again.

"Stand fast therefore in the liberty wherewith Christ hath made us free, and be not entangled again with the yoke of bondage." Galatians 5:1

Now then, let me first remind you of WHO you are…

YOU WERE CREATED IN THE IMAGE OF GOD.

"So, God created man in his own image, in the image of God created he him; male and female created he them." Genesis 1:27

YOU ARE HIS CHOSEN ONE.

"Ye have not chosen me, but I have chosen you, and ordained you, that ye should go and bring forth fruit and that your fruit should remain: that whatsoever ye shall ask of the Father in my name, he may give it you." John 15:16

YOU ARE THE APPLE OF GOD'S EYE.

"For thus saith the Lord of hosts; after the glory hath he sent me unto the nations which spoiled you: for he that toucheth you toucheth the apple of his eye." Zechariah 2:8

While in the center of the forty-month heart shattering church conflict, each day greeted us with an unexpected attack from the six employees. Television, radio, newspapers and social media sadly neglected to exercise due diligence in reporting the truth.

The profuse agony we endured left many scars, but the most catastrophic was knowing our children would be scarred as well. Our children were young and in school at the time, and their classmates began to express the harsh opinions of their parents, which caused us to search for a safe and non-judgmental environment for our children to grow academically. We eventually settled on a private school over 20 miles from our home. We felt a sense of peace, and enrolled our four children: one in high school, two in middle school and one in elementary school.

It was a frigid overcast Wednesday morning. We were driving the children to school and, unbeknownst to me, it would document itself as one of the most difficult days in our lives. We strapped the kindergartner into his booster seat, and made sure the other children were nestled in their seatbelts. They were given the books we wanted them to read that morning, while we turned on the Christian tunes of Gospel Radio. Instead of music, we heard the host announce, "Mega Church Pastor Joel Peebles ousted from his church, following the death of his mother, Apostle Betty Peebles." We were able to successfully divert the children's attention and changed the station to an R&B Morning Show. They, too, were reporting the same, but this time the children simultaneously belted out, "Mom and Dad, what are they talking about?" We told them not to worry and to continue reading their books. We turned the station a third time, only to hear that host covering our story as well.

Piercing into one another's eyes, but remaining silent, my husband and I each unerringly knew what the other was thinking, and he turned the car around and drove us back home. We were now faced with deciding how to explain what happened in a way that didn't cause our children to be angry with nor disappointed in the people who left us for dead. We knew we had to handle this delicately, as we both understood this would determine the type of relationship our children would ultimately have with God.

When we arrived home, I had a sit-down with my eldest son and namesake of his father, Joel Jr., and during our sit-down, Joel said something that completely ungrounded me. He said, "Mommy, I don't like how you and Dad are handling things during this church battle." Before I reacted to his harsh statement, I told him that he owed me an explanation really fast. My son said, "You and Dad are so busy praying and fasting for the individuals that have done this to you and it's not working. You are busy teaching love to the members of the church and it's not working. They are winning. Every time we go to court, they win. Don't you see? What you and Dad are doing is not working. So, I don't want to follow God."

Hearing that nearly destroyed me. I grabbed my chest and prayed a quick prayer. I then thought to myself, we are not preachers of the Gospel for any other reason than we really believe in God and we want others to believe in and follow Him as well. I turned away from my son and begged God to give me the right words. God said, "Turn back around!" And I said, "But I don't know what to say." Once again, God exclaimed, "Turn back around and face your son." My thoughts discombobulated and my emotions engulfed me. I begged God, "Please, give me the words to help my son understand that You are in ultimate control and that it shall be well." For the third time God persisted, "TURN BACK AROUND." I acquiesced, looked at my son, and softly whispered, "I don't know how and I don't know when; BUT, I know as sure as I stand in front of you Joel Robert Peebles Jr., that God will vindicate this situation. That, I know for certain!" Then I hugged him and I leisurely walked away.

The following year, and on a morning in November 2013, our son was home for Thanksgiving break from his freshman year of college. He walked into my powder room and said, "Hey Mom, good morning. I'm headed out to pick up breakfast for my siblings, so you don't have to cook." I placed my hand on his forehead and prayed, "I plead The Blood of Jesus over you." "Okay mom, I know, I know, Jesus…Jesus…Jesus," he said, a bit sarcastically. Even then, he was still struggling with his relationship with Christ and those who professed to be Christians but had unapologetically wounded us.

Exactly forty-two minutes later, my husband received a phone call informing him that our son's car was hit head-on, flipped three times and landed in a ditch. He was being rushed to the nearest hospital. When we arrived on the scene, looking at his car, our knees virtually buckled, but we made it back to our car to head to the hospital. Once arriving at the hospital, the surgeon wasted no time in coming to greet us. "Mr. and Mrs. Peebles," he said, "It's customary for us to receive images of accidents such as this. It gives us an idea of what we may have to handle when a patient arrives. When I see images like your son's accident, I immediately prepare myself to cut open their chest, to keep them alive. Now follow me."

"No sir, please tell me what's happening with our son!" "Just follow me," he restated. I begged him, "Doctor, I need to be prepared before I see my son. I need a moment to pray." He eagerly blurts out, "Follow me," and opened the double doors. On the other side of the double doors was the recovery room, where our son was all smiles, and simply said, "Hey Mom and Dad, all I have is a severe scratch on my left hand and leg."

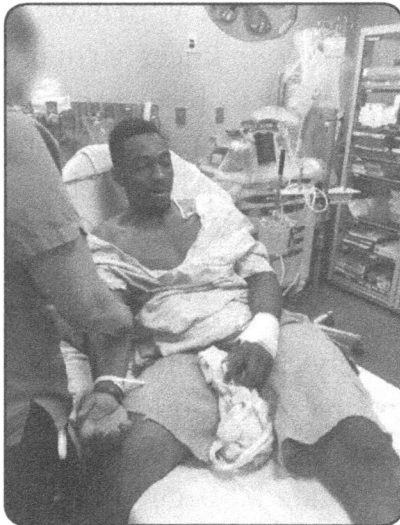

YOU KNOW WHAT TIME IT IS… A PRAISE BREAK! GOOD GOD ALMIGHTY! IF ONLY I HAD A THOUSAND TONGUES, I STILL COULDN'T PRAISE HIM ENOUGH!

Okay, I'm back!

It's those glorious moments when nothing else matters. And I mean NOTHING! The cares of the world vanished and all that filled my universe was GRATITUDE. God allowed our son to survive a nearly fatal accident.

Soon after walking through the door, bringing our son home from the hospital, my husband's cell phone rings again, and bracing ourselves, he answers. This time it's our attorney in the church case. The attorney asked my husband if I was nearby and cautioned us both to sit down. My response was, O*h Lord, every time someone says sit down it's disconcerting news. Just tell us, with The Grace of God; we can handle it.* He eagerly replied, "Trust me, you're going to want to sit down." After what seemed like an infinity, he joyfully bellowed, "I just want you to know that we hit a slam dunk and the courts have issued an order stating you can return to your church." With no exchange of words, we LITERALLY grabbed each other and rolled around endlessly on the hardwood floor in the foyer of our home.

OUR GOD IS ABLE! AND HIS CHILDREN ARE DESERVING OF HIS BEST!

In less than a twenty-four-hour period, God spared our son's life and vindicated us from the forty months of painstakingly brutal hurt, lies and misrepresentation. God did not fail us. He did precisely what His Word said He would do. We made a CHOICE to allow UNCONDITIONAL LOVE to lead us and to abide in His Word; and Beloved, there are benefits to obedience.

"He that dwelleth in the secret place of the most High shall abide under the shadow of the Almighty. I will say of the Lord, He is my refuge and my fortress: my God; in him will I trust. Surely he shall deliver thee from the snare of the fowler, and from the noisome pestilence. He shall cover thee with his feathers, and under his wings shalt thou trust: his truth shall be thy shield and buckler. Thou shalt not be afraid for the terror by night; nor for the arrow that flieth by day: Nor for the pestilence that walketh in darkness; nor for the destruction that wasteth at noonday. A thousand shall fall at thy side, and ten thousand at thy right hand; but it shall not come nigh thee. Only with thine eyes shalt thou behold and see the reward of the wicked. Because thou hast made the Lord, which is my refuge; even the most High, thy habitation; There shall no evil befall thee, neither shall any plague come nigh thy dwelling. For he shall give his angels charge over them, to keep thee in all thy ways. They shall bear thee up in their hands, lest thou dash thy foot against a stone. Thou shalt tread upon the lion and adder: the young lion and the dragon shalt thou trample under feet. Because he hath set his love upon me, therefore will I deliver him: I will set him on high, because

he hath known my name. He shall call upon me, and I will answer him: I will be with him in trouble: I will deliver him, and honor him. With long life will I satisfy him, and shew him my salvation." Psalm 91

Someone needed that entire passage of scripture, and NOW you need a moment to give Him Praise, for His Promises are Yea and Amen.

"For all the promises of God in Him are yea and in Him Amen, unto the glory of God through us." II Corinthians 1:20

I remain flabbergasted by the manifestation of God's Love, and I CELEBRATE NOW FOR YOUR WINNING SEASON!!!

YOU ARE WORTHY OF GOD'S BEST, and when the breakthrough comes, don't think more highly of yourself nor boast in the fall of your offenders. CHOOSE to continue walking in God's Will and God's Way, or there are much heavier consequences to pay.

"Woe to you, teachers of the law and Pharisees, you hypocrites! You travel over land and sea to win a single convert, and when you have succeeded, you make them twice as much a child of hell as you are." Matthew 23:15

This was given to us by God, during our darkest hour, and as a family, we professed it every evening before bed. To date, we continue to pray this prayer, and perhaps it will be a blessing to you and your family.

Dear God, we pray and thank You for: Wisdom, Power, Great Health, Peace, Prosperity and Strength. Victory, Vindication and Validation. In the Name of our Lord and Savior, Jesus Christ we pray. Amen. That finishes it! It's sealed in Your Blood!

FOCUS SCRIPTURE:

"The steps of a man are ordered by the LORD who takes delight in his journey. Though he falls, he will not be overwhelmed, for the LORD is holding his hand. I once was young and now am old, yet never have I seen the righteous abandoned or their children begging for bread. They are ever generous and quick to lend, and their children are a blessing."
Psalm 37:23-26

CALL TO ACTION:

Go through the Bible and write out as many scriptures that affirm your value, worthiness and identity in God. Let the Holy Spirit take you on a self-discovery through the scriptures.

CHAPTER 6

Forgive to be Free

Decorating the sky with its delicate dominance and visible boldness, the eagle takes its graceful voyage through life, unbothered by any imminent danger. It's direct, assertive, and motivated by achievement. It epitomizes POWER, STRENGTH, and FREEDOM.

Face to face with a catastrophic storm, it is wise enough to use the wind, confident enough to fly directly in, prudent enough to accept the pressure, ultimately never having to waste its own energy. You are that EAGLE that flies at an altitude too high to stay attached to bitterness and unforgiveness. You are that EAGLE that's POWERFUL enough to overcome every adversity. You are that EAGLE that's STRONG enough to *Get Off the Ferris Wheel of Self-Destruction*. You are that EAGLE that's too FREE to entangle yourself with the yokes of bondage again.

YOU ARE THAT EAGLE!
I AM THAT EAGLE!
WE ARE THAT EAGLE!

It was the summer of 2012, and we were headed out for a family road trip, a much-welcomed break for just a few days. The anticipation of the escape filled our hearts with joy. While humming the tunes of peaceful jazz melodies, we packed our luggage for this short but highly anticipated trip, when I reminded myself that this was the time of year that I normally fasted and prayed for a week. This time, however, I would delay it until we returned.

The next morning, we loaded the family minivan with so much luggage, one would think we were leaving indefinitely. Intentionally CHOOSING to leave our cares with God, we departed from our home with this scripture in mind:

"Cast all your anxiety on him because he cares for you."
I Peter 5:7

As we drove up to the quaint and secluded resort, different shades of bliss danced through our hearts. I began to reflect on pieces of a poem that I adore, written by Alyssa Underwood, entitled, "The Joyful Heart."

"The joyful heart is the buoyant heart –
empowered to rise above its circumstances,
unweighted, unburdened, unbound,
tied only to that which would lift it higher,
untethered from anything which would
pull it down, pull it under or suffocate it.

It's the free heart, quiet and at rest
yet jubilant and uncontained,
the celebrating heart, the praising heart,

the thankful heart, the heart set on pilgrimage,
bent on adventure, journey and romance..."

For this trip, I surrendered to the process of letting go, and I decided to enjoy every moment. I then turned to the children, asleep in the back of the minivan, and began to pray that this trip would be a time to enjoy one another. Truly, I wanted us all to leave the cares of the church battle far behind.

As we waited patiently in the minivan, my fine, wonderful, and incredible husband went to check us in. I gazed out the window, cheerfully smiling with overwhelming anticipation for what was ahead, and the weight of my heaviness evaporated into the still air. My thoughts settled on the comforts of:

"Therefore I say unto you, take no thought for your life, what
ye shall eat, or what ye shall drink; nor yet for your body,
what ye shall put on. Is not the life more than meat, and
the body than raiment? Behold the fowls of the air: for they
sow not, neither do they reap, nor gather into barns; yet your
heavenly Father feedeth them. Are ye not much better than
they? Which of you by taking thought can add one cubit unto
his stature? And why take ye thought for raiment? Consider
the lilies of the field, how they grow; they toil not, neither do
they spin: And yet I say unto you, that even Solomon in all
his glory was not arrayed like one of these. Wherefore, if God
so clothe the grass of the field, which today is, and tomorrow
is cast into the oven, shall he not much more clothe you, O ye
of little faith? Therefore, take no thought, saying, what shall
we eat? Or, what shall we drink? Or, wherewithal shall

we be clothed? For after all these things do the Gentiles seek: for your heavenly Father knoweth that ye have need of all these things. But seek ye first the kingdom of God, and his righteousness: and all these things shall be added unto you."
Matthew 6:25–33

Following a full day of amusing activities, the evening drew late, so we enjoyed a peaceful dinner on the resort lanai, with the breeze echoing God's Sentiments of Love. No thoughts of the church battle, health reports, financial loss, truth assassinations, brokenness, nor heartache... NOTHING! This was yet another opportunity to move out of God's Way, and allow Him to do what He does so prolifically: VINDICATE and VALIDATE.

"No weapon that is formed against thee shall prosper; and every tongue that shall rise against thee in judgment thou shalt condemn. This is the heritage of the servants of the Lord, and their righteousness is of me, saith the Lord." Isaiah 54:17

We settled in for the evening at approximately midnight; but at 5:00 AM, God woke me up with, "Ylawnda! Today is the day!" You can imagine my astonishment. "Today's the day you work on self-love!" More puzzled, I said, "What do you mean Lord?" He was crystal clear, "I want you to pray and forgive, which is the greatest expression of self-love. Pray and forgive the individuals who have violated you, your family, and church family." I threw my hands up to surrender. "I'll do exactly what You instruct me to, but I'll do it as soon as we get back home." He whispered, "You'll pray right *now*. Right *here*, right *now*."

Was this essentially my assignment, at 5:00 AM, on the solid hotel room floor? I ceased from hesitating, and complied. On the floor, I stretched out a few towels and laid prostrate. Upon saying, "Father, in The Name Lord Jesus," God said, "There are a few more instructions."

I digress to inform you that God does undeniably speak, and I'll delightfully prove it to you, using the brilliant explanation my husband gives when he ministers. "You know those times when you want to slap your supervisor, but a still, small voice advises you against it? That's God speaking."

Sometimes we are deaf to His Voice because we aren't in the proper spiritual alignment to listen. Even as I type this chapter, I know God speaks. I have history with God speaking to me. Yet, I ask myself, how many times have I been deaf to His Voice because I was too busy working, too busy taking care of others, too busy making plans, even too busy in my own feelings? God irrefutably speaks, but the question is, are we sitting still long enough to listen?

"My sheep hear my voice, and I know them, and they follow me: And I give unto them eternal life; and they shall never perish, neither shall any man pluck them out of my hand."
John 10:27-28

I sat up on the floor to attentively listen to all of God's instructions. He said my prayer assignment wasn't for one day, but for *thirty consecutive* days.

Yes, it resembled cruel and unusual punishment, not a self-love assignment. However, I continued to be still and listen. I was charged with praying an extremely specific prayer on my enemy's behalf. God said, "Call out each name and ask Me to bless them, their children, and their children's children. Ask Me to be a covering over their health and finances. Ask Me to grant them peace and joy."

Wait! What?! This was clearly a toilsome test that left me contemplating if it was actually God speaking or if it was the devil. So, I put God in remembrance of His Word in an attempt to be freed from this agonizing assignment. God, Your Word says, *"The effectual fervent prayer of a righteous man availeth much" James 5:16,* and if I comply with what You are asking, seeing them walk in this type of breakthrough blessing, while we yet bleed…it's too much God! Too much!!!!" God's response was, "When you finish venting, do exactly what I instructed you to do!"

I began praying exactly as He charged me. I called out their individual names, and asked God to bless them, bless their children, and their children's children. I asked Him to cover their health and finances, as well as grant them peace and blessings. I genuinely prayed with my whole heart.

I was certain it was an hour and fifteen minutes later. I sat up, looked at my watch, and stared in disbelief; *Only seven minutes?!* How would I do this for fifty-three more minutes, and not to mention, twenty-nine more days?! This was torture; but there was no escaping. I completed the one-hour prayer and committed to the assignment for twenty-nine more days. With this daunting assignment, we still treasured our brief but wonderful getaway.

Back at home, it was now two weeks into the thirty days, and while sitting in our chairs in our bedroom suite, I turned to my husband and said, "It's time for my one-hour prayer; would you care to join me?" With an intense and prolonged stare, he responds, "No! You're a better man than me." We both literally laughed out loud. As I was headed down to our prayer room, God corrected me, and told me that He didn't call my husband to this assignment. He had enough responsibility to bear, in covering his family and church family. This was not his assignment; it was mine, and I continued downstairs.

At the conclusion of the thirty days, just like our lives, some days are painstakingly difficult, while on others, we skip with glee. I took out my journal, walked out on the deck, and there to welcome me was a beautiful small bird with a red tipped tail.

I envisioned the Blood of Jesus and the tranquility of God covering me as I reminded myself of Noah.

"After forty days, Noah opened a window he had made in the ark and sent out a raven, and it kept flying back and forth until the water had dried up from the earth. Then he sent out a dove to see if the water had receded from the surface of the ground. But the dove could find nowhere to perch because there was water over all the surface of the earth; so it returned to Noah in the ark. He reached out his hand and took the dove and brought it back to himself in the ark. He waited seven more days and again sent out the dove from the ark. When the dove returned to him in the evening, there in its beak was a freshly plucked olive leaf! Noah knew that the water had receded from the earth. He waited seven more days and sent the dove out again, but this time it did not return to him. By the first day of the first month of Noah's six hundred and first year, the water had dried up from the earth. Noah then removed the covering from the ark and saw that the surface of

the ground was dry. By the twenty-seventh day of the second month the earth was completely dry." Genesis 8:6-13

IT'S THAT TIME AGAIN…I HAVE TO RUN, SHOUT, PRAISE, DANCE AND GLORIFY MY GOD!

Okay, I'm back!!!

Like Noah, God had sent me a sign. In the natural, things remained the same, but in the Spirit, EVERYTHING CHANGED! I scurried into the house to locate my phone to capture the moment in picture, and God allowed the Red Robin to sit on the ledge of my deck, just long enough for me to understand the message and take a picture.

The actual picture I took on the deck of my home.

When you CHOOSE to crucify your flesh and obey The Will of God, there is unequivocally a REWARD.

"And Samuel said, Hath the Lord as great delight in burnt offerings and sacrifices, as in obeying the voice of the Lord? Behold, to obey is better than sacrifice..." I Samuel 15:22

Be willing to humble yourself and seek God's Face. Doing so has its rewards, but they don't mysteriously rain down from the clouds above. They don't often present themselves when we wish them to; however, they are right on time. We didn't see the manifestation of the breakthrough in that month, that year, or the next, or the next, but God did manifest it in His pre-ordained time. Remember, never move in front of God and don't move behind Him. Let Him lead and guide you.

"Howbeit when he, the Spirit of truth, is come, he will guide you into all truth: for he shall not speak of himself; but whatsoever he shall hear, that shall he speak: and he will shew you things to come..." John 16:13

God never loses control of your situation. Love yourself enough to let go and FORGIVE. Holding on damages your soul, purpose, destiny, and that of the generations behind you. Be willing to obey God when He asks, and do it exactly how He says.

Do not have a begrudging spirit when He asks you to make a sacrifice, because true sacrifice is obedience. Loving yourself is not in the sculpture of your eyebrows, the length of your lashes, the manicured nails, and flawless hair; but it is in your obedience. Go ahead, give yourself permission to paint the sky with your individual signature of Self-Love, by walking in obedience, forgiveness and holiness.

FOCUS SCRIPTURE:

"And whenever you stand praying, forgive, if you have anything against anyone, so that your Father also who is in heaven may forgive you your trespasses…" Mark 11:25

CALL TO ACTION:

For ten days, sacrifice thirty minutes to pray for those who have hurt you. Ask the Holy Spirit to guide you and to give you strength. You will need it.

CHAPTER 7
Give Yourself Permission to Live

V incent van Gogh's *"The Starry Night"* is one of the most recognized pieces of art in the world; *"Ode to Joy,"* Beethoven's 9th Symphony; *"The Clarinet Concerto,"* one of Mozart's best loved works. Each of these prolific works of art resonate as a testament to how its beauty is timeless and universal. From the first stroke of the paintbrush to the final note of a magnificent composition, it's all impressively crafted in a space, called "TIME."

Theoretical physicists, Albert Einstein and Carlo Rovelli, say, "Time is an illusion. It is relative." The ancient Greeks defined time in two words: *chronos*, referring to chronological or sequential time, and *kairos*, signifying a proper or opportune time for action. Chronos is *quantitative*, and kairos is *qualitative*.

We can agree to disagree on our theory of time. However, I would beg to argue that "time," as we know it now, is both precious and limited.

"To every thing there is a season and a time to every purpose under the heaven: A time to be born, and a time to die; a time to plant, and a time to pluck up that which is planted; A time

to kill, and a time to heal; a time to break down, and a time to build up; A time to weep, and a time to laugh; a time to mourn, and a time to dance; A time to cast away stones, and a time to gather stones together; a time to embrace, and a time to refrain from embracing; A time to get, and a time to lose; a time to keep, and a time to cast away; A time to rend, and a time to sew; a time to keep silence, and a time to speak; A time to love, and a time to hate; a time of war, and a time of peace..." Ecclesiastes 3:1-8

God has privileged us with the gift of time, and we must CHOOSE to use it wisely.

"I must work the works of him that send me, while it is day: the night cometh, when no man can work." John 9:4

BREATHE. TRUST. HOPE. LOVE. FORGIVE. By all means, JUST LIVE!

Take every opportunity to cherish and live in the moment. Take every opportunity to be good to others. Take every opportunity to extend forgiveness, grace and mercy. Take every opportunity to love unconditionally. JUST LIVE!

As time drifts by, life seems to move at a more rapid pace. Few find it necessary to enjoy the innocence of life, like baking a cake or growing your own garden. Enjoy the long, scenic route instead of the shortcut; cooking your food instead of putting it in the microwave; learning a basic hemming stitch, as opposed to using hemming tape.

Slow down enough to LIVE and create memories, so that when you are old, you have no regrets in retrospect.

You're reading this book for a reason much bigger than yourself. Our destinies are always much bigger than anything we could ever dream, so it's time to LIVE. It's time to stop, breathe, and simply be in the moment.

It was December of 1998. With the earthy smell of Autumn filling the air and the vibrant leaves falling like rain to the ground, our youngest son Jordan, two weeks old, developed a fever. He began coughing uncontrollably and had difficulty breathing. I gave him pain and allergy medicine, along with a breathing treatment. However, nothing made an impact, and we ultimately decided to take him to the doctor. After a brief examination, medication was prescribed, but that didn't provide relief.

On the third day, the fever persisted, and his breathing was visibly labored. We rushed him back to the doctor's office, where she requested an x-ray. The doctor was alarmed with the results and requested a second x-ray. Unaware that an ambulance had been called, we stood in shock hearing he would be raced to a local Children's Hospital.

Upon his arrival, his breathing was so labored that his tiny body would slightly lift out of my arms with each inhale. I handed the baby to my husband to run to the powder room. On my way back to my husband and baby, what looked like an army of white coats walked rapidly towards us. It was then explained that Jordan's right lung had collapsed, and he would need emergency surgery. We were told it was a tremendously painful surgery, with only a local anesthetic, due to his age. No explanation given made any logical sense as to how this could have happened, as he was only two weeks old.

They grabbed the baby and took him to a room, stripped him of his clothes, and put him in a clear encasement which blew air into his lungs. While my husband kneeled next to the baby to pray, I stepped into the hallway and paced the floor. I blurted out, "Speak Lord! This is really difficult. I can't watch my baby struggle to breathe. "HELP!" All I heard The Lord say was, "Get another x-ray."

With my husband's back facing me, as he continued to pray next to the baby, I said, "Dad, God said to get another x-ray." For what seemed like an infinity, he didn't respond. "Dad," I said, "did you hear me? God said, 'Get another x-ray.'" He literally turned to me slowly, with such compassion, and said, "If that's what God said, let's do it."

We called for the nurse to request a third x-ray. The medical team thought it was preposterous, as they already had images of two x-rays. After much duress, they finally agreed to take the third image.

While in the hallway, waiting on the technician, the baby was struggling and it was heartbreaking to watch. It felt like forever, when a doctor finally walked toward us with a clipboard in hand, instructing us to sign some papers that stated we were refusing emergency treatment by CHOOSING to waste time in requesting a third x-ray. I cried out literally to God, asking Him, "Am I operating in fact, faith, or foolishness? I don't want the blood of my innocent baby on my hands and heart. Are you speaking? What should we do?" "Get the X-ray!" is indeed what I heard The Lord say.

Our baby stayed in the hospital for three days, still with low oxygen in his lungs, but no surgery and no explanation of how his lung had straightened on its own. With elated but anguished hearts we asked, "God, why would You allow us to go through such turmoil? We are grateful for his healing, but why such agony?" But the answer didn't come until the next day.

The night before Jordan's discharge, two doctors walked into the room with an update on his status, and in total disbelief that things turned around as they did. They explained that they had never seen anything like that before. For the next hour, we talked with them about God and His Plan of Salvation. They both confessed Jesus as their Lord and we all rejoiced.

The next morning, as Jordan was being discharged, God said, "And that's why you had to endure this anguish. I trusted you with this test, so I could get My Word to the two doctors. Well done, children, well done." My husband and I hugged one another so close and tight, then swaddled our baby in a warm blanket and took him home.

Two months later, we received a letter in the mail from both doctors, thanking us for allowing ourselves to be used by God. They stated that although we were going through a difficult situation, we still invested time to share the Love of Jesus.

Your storm is not about you, it's about the testimony God designed to get from it; a testimony that blesses you, but gives Him glory.

What will you do with your time?

You have lived through pain before and you CONQUERED!

You have lived through abandonment before and OVERCOME!

You have lived through devastation and yet you're STILL HERE!

JUST LIVE. READER, CHOOSE TO LIVE!

FOCUS SCRIPTURE:

"Blessed are you who hunger now, for you will be satisfied. Blessed are you who weep now, for you will laugh." Luke 6:21

CALL TO ACTION:

For Seven Days:

1. Go outside with a journal.
2. Close your eyes for ten minutes.
3. Listen to the sounds of nature. The patterns of the wind. Birds chirping. Moving vehicles and overhead planes.
4. Open your eyes.
5. Write down all of the good feelings that you experienced within those 10 minutes.

CHAPTER 8

Be a Woman of Transformation

One evening, while enjoying family and a group I formed called, "The Couple of Forever's Club," I asked a question— "How would you describe the color orange to a blind person?" As you can imagine, there were various responses, but the best one came from my eldest son, Joel Jr.

He walked to the front of the banquet hall in our basement and said, "Remember the day you sat in front of a warm, cozy fireplace, with the crackling sounds of the wood? Well, that's the color orange."

I thought it was the most ingenious way to describe the color orange. However, a debate ensued, and some argued there is no possible way to describe the color to someone with no vision. You see, that's indeed how God feels. We have sixty-six books of the Bible to help govern our lives; yet, we still can't see.

Transformation is part of life's journey. It can be ugly, painful and prolonged. Isn't it interesting that babies are not born with the ability to walk, talk, or care for themselves? A funny thing about that is, we don't loathe the process. Why then do we despise the process of spiritual growth? If we never collide with adversity, how do we become a better person?

"And be not conformed to this world: but be ye transformed by the renewing of your mind, that ye may prove what is that good, and acceptable, and perfect, will of God." Romans 12:2

In this chapter, I am delighted to share with you another assignment given to me by God, and the actual testimonies of those that took the journey with me.

THEY HAVE TRANSFORMED!
I HAVE TRANSFORMED!
WE HAVE TRANFORMED!
WILL YOU?!?

On January 1, 2017, which I playfully refer to as, *January the One*, the genesis of something special began. Something The Lord instructed me to do was about to change the lives of many, including myself.

I was seated on my fluffy pink powder room chair, swaying to the tunes of India Arie, and putting on mascara to accentuate my lashes. I was priming myself for date night with hubby, when God gave me yet another assignment. I heard God clearly say that He wanted me to start a Gratitude Journey. I had no idea what this meant or entailed. He instructed me to do something I had never done before. I was to log onto Facebook Live, and for anyone viewing, I was to invite them on this Journey of Gratitude. Still unsure of what this would entail, I had enough experiences with God that I wasn't going to debate Him on this one.

"Now," God said. Obediently, I turned on my phone and went live on Facebook. Apprehensively, I hit the button and history began, with twenty people tuned in. Dubious of how I was going to fit this into my demanding schedule, I explained to the viewers that I would go live for a random five minutes that I would carve out every day. Five minutes seemed to be the perfect time to give some words of inspiration and encouragement.

The next morning, *January 2nd*, I opened up the Facebook app, to see over fifteen hundred messages in my Facebook inbox. There were too many to which I could respond, but I inadvertently hit one message and decided to read it. Thank God I did.

She wrote: "My name is Mary *(name has been changed, as the author didn't want her name revealed)*, and I reside in Botswana, Africa. Shattered, broken and with no motive to continue living, I made plans to take my life this morning. I have a lot of family here, but no reason to live, so I wanted to give them a proper goodbye."

The message continued, "I opened my phone to tell them all so long, but your video popped up. It immediately caught my attention, and while watching it, I felt my life changing. How can we stay in touch? I need this type of motivation in my life."

Left speechless, I pontificated about how I wanted and needed to respond. I decided to pray before forwarding a reply and God gave the exact reassurance:

"We are hard pressed on every side, but not crushed; perplexed, but not in despair; persecuted, but not abandoned; struck down, but not destroyed." II Corinthians 4:8-9

"And the God of all grace, who called you to his eternal glory in Christ, after you have suffered a little while, will himself restore you and make you strong, firm and steadfast."
I Peter 5:10

"Peace I leave with you, my peace I give unto you: not as the world giveth, give I unto you. Let not your heart be troubled, neither let it be afraid." John 14:27

I continued with, "Ms. Mary, you are the chosen one of your Heavenly Father and He desires for you to prosper.

Beloved, I wish above all things that thou mayest prosper and be in health, even as thy soul prospereth. III John 1:2

Ms. Mary, God wants to give you a testimony, but that always precedes a test. Ms. Mary, *Nay, in all these things we are more than conquerors through him that loved us. Romans 8:37*

I pray that God allows our paths to cross and I pray that we will meet in person one day. Until then, I reserve a big hug for you. Please know, you have someone across land and sea that is praying for you, and that's me." Signed, Your Biggest Fan, Ylawnda Peebles.

In March of that same year, I hosted what I call a Gratitude Journey Celebration Bash for all the viewers. Nearly two thousand viewers, whom I affectionally call GRATITUDERS, came from near and far to attend the event. At the end of that night, after a three-hour celebration, I wanted to make certain that everyone felt loved, so I said, "If anyone needs another hug before leaving, I want to be the one to give it to you." What seemed like an endless line rapidly formed. After approximately an hour, the line began to diminish, and I noticed a woman all the way in the back of our church. She was sitting, with a desperate stare, and wailing copiously.

As I embraced the last person, she stood slowly; my eyes were glued to her as she began walking toward me. As she continued crying desolately, I moved with haste and sympathy to meet her halfway. Ultimately, when she got to me, she hugged me and collapsed in my arms. I could sense her mental exhaustion, yet her outbreath of release.

Her body weight resting on me, I attempted to hold us both up, when someone else moved in to assist us. Looking at me with such desperation and continuing to sob, she said, "I'm Ms. Mary, the lady from Botswana, Africa, who wrote you the letter." She continued, "And you saved my life. I flew over twenty hours just to lay my eyes on you." Her tears flowed from her heart as I asked, "But why?! Why would you fly this far to see me? I'm not the hero, you are the hero! You're the hero because you CHOSE to LIVE! I was simply the instrument God used to get a message of HOPE to you. I celebrate you for CHOOSING to LIVE!"

I asked my assistant to please grab me a mirror and when she did, I held the mirror up in front of Ms. Mary and said, "Look! That's a true warrior, overcomer, champion and survivor. You destroyed that enemy's plan for your life. Do you realize that?" She intensely stared into the mirror, but provided no response to my question, so I reminded her of her inner beauty and that she was worthy of living. I told her that God had a plan and a purpose for her life.

"For I know the thoughts that I think toward you, saith the Lord, thoughts of peace, and not of evil, to give you an expected end." Jeremiah 29:11

It was then that I realized, this Facebook YP Gratitude Journey was bigger than me. It was worth more than a random five minutes of my time each day. Subsequently, I went live on Facebook for one hour and a consecutive three hundred and sixty-five days, not missing a single day.

I FEEL LIKE RUNNING, SHOUTING AND DANCING AGAIN!

Only God got me through an ENTIRE year, even through the days that my life was charged with challenges. I vividly remember one particular day when my sisters drove my mother to the hospital emergency room with complaints of severe chest pains, only fifteen minutes before the live show was scheduled to air. On my way to the hospital and unsure of what to do about the show, God told me to take the viewers live with me into her hospital room, and they, too, would experience her victory. I also remember thinking, what if my faith fails, what then would I say to the Gratituders? But glory be to God, I obeyed His command, walked into that hospital room full of faith, and two hours later my mother was released.

I also recall my cousin was rushed to the hospital, and shortly after was put on life support. Oh, and what about the time a nerve in my ear tore and left me in excruciating pain. Yet, I dug deep, pulled on a lesson I often use to inspire the Gratituders, and that gave me strength and courage. And that lesson was and is today, "Stay the Course!" Every battle is a fixed fight in God; just stay the course and your victory is inevitable.

Although I am the teacher, inspirer, motivator, *(warmly called the Chief Gratituder by the viewers)*, I, too, am a student. When God is speaking about the lesson for the day, I am a student. When I go live, I am then, the teacher, inspirer, and motivator. I have been consistently clear that I cannot teach lessons that I'm not willing to walk through myself, and seeing the transformation within me and the Gratituders has been nothing short of exceptional.

Beloved, God is no respecter of persons, and if He can FREE Ms. Mary, if He can FREE me, if He can FREE the Gratituders, then He can surely FREE you, too.

"For there is no respect of person with God." Romans 2:11

FOCUS SCRIPTURE:

"For You formed my inmost being; You knit me together in my mother's womb. I praise You, for I am fearfully and wonderfully made. Marvelous are Your works, and I know this very well." Psalm 139:13-14

CALL TO ACTION:

Join us on the #YPGratitudeJourney live on Facebook, every Tuesday and Thursday at 7:00pm EST, and I promise you this, "Your Life will Never Ever Be the Same Again!"

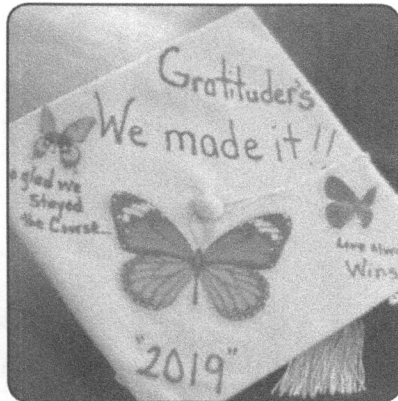

This was our Gratituders' Graduation, first in the history of the world.

CHAPTER 9

Get Your Wings and Fly

The grandiose horizon awaits you. Postpone it no longer, but discover it. The air you shall breathe there is that of love and freedom; why wait?! The wonders of INTREPID HOPE were always the route to your destination; why stagger? The weight of your baggage is all that will stifle you, so, "MAKE A MORE EXCELLENT CHOICE!"

Not all flights have turbulence, but those are actually the ones that build your strength and integrity; why run?! It was never intended to destroy you, but to make you all the WISER. Your dreams, your vision, your destiny, all have wings. Accept the flight, and enjoy your new life.

During the second year of the *#YPGratitudeJourney*, I asked all the Gratituders to write a letter for what I deemed, *Testimony Tuesday*, to express how this journey has impacted their lives, and the lives of those around them. The heartfelt letters poured in.

There is no other conceivable way to discuss "Getting Wings and Flying," other than through the real time, unedited testimonies of those who lived it, and these are their actual letters:

On Tue, Nov 6, 2018, 10:55 AM Ericka wrote:

Good morning, Pastor!

I apologize in advance for this being so long but I need to get it out.

Last week, you talked about the worst thing that ever happened to us. I talked about my mother leaving me at the age of 10. My mother left me with my grandmother at the babysitter with all of my clothes/shoes and most of my toys with a note for my grandmother saying, "YOU WANT HER YOU GOT HER". She moved to North Carolina. A few years later, she returned with a baby. My first little brother. I was supposed to be happy. She asked if I wanted to hold him. I told her I don't want it. I was so angry and hurt that she left ME and went off and had another baby. What was wrong with me?!?! It took me YEARS to build self-esteem. I was well into my 20's. I felt so worthless and unwanted.

My mother never liked me. She was always jealous of the relationship I have/had with my grandmother. She used to hit me, punch me, lock me in the bedroom when she had male company....I had to bang on the door to use the bathroom and many times I could not hold it so I was beaten for urinating on myself. To this day she is still jealous.

My grandmother raised ALL FOUR of her kids. My brothers are drug babies and have mental illnesses such as bipolar disorder, autism, paranoid schizophrenia, and ADHD. I myself suffer with bipolar disorder but I was not a drug baby. I'm the only one who was not. She was, maybe still is, on drugs. I don't have much contact with her but since starting the Journey I have since told her that I am preparing myself to take her to dinner and talk about everything on my mind.

I am afraid of thunder and lightning. When I was small, she and her best friend took me to the airport to look at the planes because I've always been fascinated by planes. Well, a thunderstorm came up and I started crying and begging her to let me call my grandmother. She slapped me so hard my little sunglasses flew off. I dropped the candy she had bought me and I broke out into hives (that's what I did when I was scared or had been beaten). All because I wanted to call my grandmother because I was afraid. That's just the tip of the iceberg Pastor. You'd be reading for days if I continue.

Thanks for letting me vent.

On Nov 29, 2018, at 1:06 PM, Dana wrote:

Good afternoon, Pastor,

How are you feeling? I just want to thank you. I joined the Gratituders journey on your birthday. When you made that quote your life will never ever be the same again that is so true and it came to pass. I have learned a lot from you pastor. One thing is how to forgive, I us to fight with that thing. Holding it in and mad in the inside and a fake smile on the outside. But now that I no better, I do better and I had to ask god to forgive me first and then I had to forgive everyone that wrong me or may have hurt me, but thank you pastor.

On Tue, Dec 10, 2019, at 9:22 AM, Malika wrote:

Grateful is an understatement right now. I don't think there is a word that can truly describe what I feel right now.

All I can say is thank you! I just picked up my second book client. I am an official publisher! I got to speak at my first seminar, which lead to receiving 7 social media clients! I'm not rich yet, but I feel like I hit the lottery!!! Better than that, I feel like God heard my prayers...and once I let go of the garbage, I am free to move in the gifts that laid dormant for so long!!! SUDDENLY EVERYTHING I EVER DREAMED OF IS COMING TO PASS!

I'm apologizing for always completing your sentences...I just get so excited about the words flying out of your mouth. I know they are from heaven. I know your heart is for everyone to know this freedom!!! THANK YOU!!! FOR NOT BEING THE AVERAGE FIRST LADY... THANK YOU FOR NOT DOING "CHURCH" AS USUAL. THANK YOU FOR SHOWING ME I COULD PARTY WITHOUT THE DRUGS, ALCOHOL, AND MEN AND HAVE EVEN MORE FUN...I GET HIGH OFF OF LIFE NOW!!! I'M SITTING AT MY DESK WITH THE TEARS POURING OUT MY FACE BECAUSE GOD BROUGHT ME TO THE BEST CHURCH ON THE PLANET...AND THE BEST PEOPLE ON THE PLANET. I DIDN'T HAVE THE PERFECT LIFE OR MARRIAGE BUT I SERVE A PERFECT GOD WHO NEVER FORGOT ABOUT ME. THANK YOU FOR NOT FORGETTING ABOUT ME. I LOVE YOU SO MUCH. THESE TEARS OF JOY...GOD HAS SENT ME SOME PEOPLE WHO REALLY HAVE MY BACK...AND ITS MY DUTY TO BRING YOU A RETURN ON YOUR INVESTMENT!!!

On Dec 26, 2019, at 8:10 PM, Charles wrote:

I wanted to share my gratitude for the Gratitude Journey with my pastor Ylawnda Peebles. She has encouraged me to continue to grow and be strong thru all life challenges, and no matter what to never quit. My Pastor Ylawnda and My Bishop Joel Peebles are the closes examples of Jesus I know, no matter how anyone treated them and despite the fact we fought with them for 7 long years to get the church back from people that tried to steal it, they always said with no anger that they still love the people that harmed them and that there faith in God will give them our Church Back and to God be the Glory it came to Past, WON'T HE DO IT ???

Wed, May 30, 2018, 11:53 AM, Sylvia wrote:

Good Evening Pastor Ylawnda, Chief Gratituder

I am sending my testimony because I believe you stated that is our compensation for our journey.

I am extremely grateful for this gratitude journey!! I was invited by Jacklyn Talley Mobley and I am so grateful for her friendship. I started late January. At the time I was going through a very challenging time on my job and the only thing I was grateful for during that time was the opportunity to leave that job. God had granted me grace to start a full-time Master's in Nursing Program at University of Maryland in November 2017. I didn't know at the time how challenging it was going to be, I just knew that this was where I was supposed to be during this season in my life. I was blessed with my VA benefits, a part-time job as a Teaching Assistant and a Scholarship! What did I have to complain about? Nothing. Through the gratitude journey, I am learning to keep my eyes on Jesus, I am becoming more humble, grateful, and thankful! I have learned that when I take my eyes off of Him, I am not grateful and I start looking at what He is doing in someone else's life. When I am supposed to celebrate with others, I find that is when envy and jealousy start to creep in, even though I don't speak it out, due to shame, because really I am supposed to be a Christian right? It doesn't happen all the time, but in finding out who I really am, when no one is looking, God showed me it is an issue that needed to be dealt with. I have also learned that it is not really about that other person, because at my core, I really desire to celebrate them, it's really about my displeasure with my own life (my own issues), my own selfishness, which makes it a complaint to God! That is sin in itself. Again what do I have to complain or be envious about? Pastor Ylawnda, when you talked about getting off the Ferris Wheel, letting it go, how bad do I want it! Who am I really when no one is looking? This hit me the most, who is my authentic self? I desire to be completely free and I want God to keep showing me, me and pull those things out that are not like Him. Gratitude is one of the ways I am going to do that. I have started to ask God now to bless others even more because I want to starve this issue. I want to be just me, who God made me and love it and love others just the way they are and see their future in Jesus. I am grateful for this journey. I am trying each morning 12 times and some moments become very misty, I love it.

P.S I attended the Woman's Experience last year and honestly from there, my life has never been the same!! I was already in a season of getting to know myself and that experience just pushed me further on my journey. Sorry, I am not a member of COPFM but I believe God uses who He desires for our growth and I will forever be connected to COPFM. Thank you so much for your obedience.

In Christ Love

FOCUS SCRIPTURE:

"It is for freedom that Christ has set us free. Stand firm, then, and do not let yourselves be burdened again by a yoke of slavery." Galatians 5:1

CALL TO ACTION:

Go to a quiet place, turn on classical jazz, and write a letter to your future "FREE" self. No stipulation, just remember, it's to the FREE you.

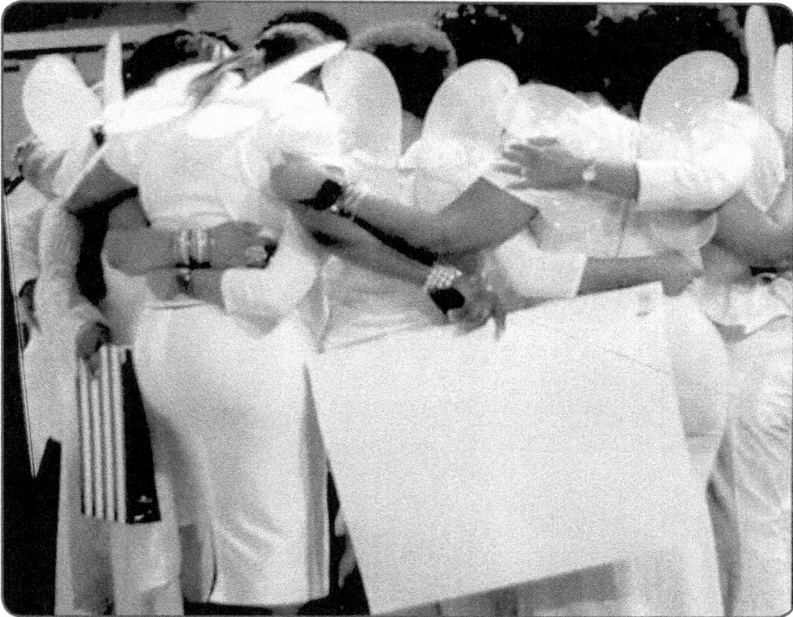

Picture taken during a Gratituders' Celebration Bash when I issued over four thousand women their FREEDOM WINGS.

CHAPTER 10
Let It All Go

Who could hold onto you? Like ice cream, you stick like bread and butter. The throbbing cavity is evidence that you're just too sweet to adore. Oh yes, you are so cool, smooth, and refreshing, that I neglect to remember just how unhealthy you are for me. For too long, I held onto you, like a moth to a flame, and ruthlessly burned.

Why then, would anyone hold onto you? Like ice cream, you MUST melt away in the sand; vanish like a bat upon the rising of the sun; fall to the ground like the earth with no gravity. You are no good for us.

What's that thing that prevents you from showing up in the world as the FREE you? What are the things that you've hidden to protect yourself from the opinions of others? LET IT GO! Whatever it is that stifles you, it will never be worth the pain, lack of peace or loss of relationships. It's costing you too much…LET IT GO!

This book was inspired by my real time and real life. There are no embellishments in my testimonies; no ghost writer. I literally invested over ten hours a day, praying, hearing from God and writing, so I pray it inspires you enough to move from where you are and agree to become all God intended. You have already taken the fundamental nine steps *(the previous nine chapters)*, to get to this point. Now congratulate yourself. Well done! Well done!

This Final Chapter is a "Celebration of Your Freedom!" If I am never privileged with an opportunity to meet you in person, please know that I declare myself to be your "Biggest Fan." Across states and countries, I shall pray for you daily, celebrate you from afar and be that whisper in your ear, reminding you to embrace the FREE YOU.

You have no idea who you really are, until you are FREE.

Salma Hayek may have coined it best, "People often say that 'beauty is in the eye of the beholder,' and I say that the most liberating thing about beauty is realizing that you are the beholder. This empowers us to find beauty in places where others have not dared to look, including inside ourselves."

MAY YOU, RIGHT NOW, DISCOVER THE BEAUTY WITHIN YOU!
MAY OTHERS UNDERSTAND THE BEAUTY OF GOD THROUGH YOU!

As I make my exit from these writings, I sincerely desire for you to know that, "MY LOVE WILL ALWAYS FIND ITS WAY TO YOUR HEART." And I leave you with Words of Affirmation and a few of my Infamous Inspiration Quotes that have been notable on the #YPGratitudeJourney:

WORDS OF AFFIRMATION

- Today, I will embrace my inner strength and realize that nothing which presents itself in my life is insurmountable. I was born a winner. I live as a winner and I will always be a winner.

- Today, I nurture healthy relationships and separate from the ones which are poisonous.

- Right now, I feel like smiling. I will CHOOSE to feel the same way in another five minutes.

- Time to grow and nurture my gift.

- I am taking an inventory of my thoughts. Those which are Godly and positive can stay, but those which are hurtful are being evicted, and I'm changing the locks.

- Today, I will pay it forward and do something kind for others. I will purchase three small inexpensive gifts and bless those who work behind the scenes.

INFAMOUS QUOTES OF INSPIRATION

"Your Life Will Never Ever, Never Ever Be The Same Again"

"Rise Up, Soldier"

"Make Love Your First Choice"

"How Bad Do You Want It"

"May Your Sleep Be Sweet"

"Hoddie Hoddie Whoooo"

"Come On With The Come On And Go 'Head With The Go 'Head"

FOCUS SCRIPTURE:

"Let your light so shine before men, that they may see your good works, and glorify your Father which is in heaven."
Matthew 5:16

CALL TO ACTION:

Congratulations, Beloved! You made it to the last action of this book. Now, for your final Call to Action:

1. Get something tangible in your hand that reminds you of your deepest pain.
2. Write a short letter about that pain.
3. Throw the letter in a place where it cannot be recovered. You can't be free holding onto the things that God intended for you to let go.
4. Bake a small cake. It doesn't have to be perfect.
5. Put "SEVEN" candles on the cake *(7 represents complete VICTORY).*
6. Extinguish your candles.

Give God Praise!

And there you have it, TRANSFORMATION! METAMORPHOSIS! THE BEST VERSION OF YOU.

DON'T RUN FROM THE DIFFICULT TIMES.
THEY ARE DESIGNED TO BUILD YOUR FAITH
AND CHARACTER. LOVE THE SKIN YOU'RE IN
AND CHOOSE TO WIN!

Copious Love,
Your Biggest Fan
Pastor Ylawnda Peebles, D.D., D.H.L.

A WOMAN OF GRACE, POISE & EXCELLENCE

Ylawnda Peebles is the exultant wife of 27 years to her best friend, Senior Pastor, Joel R. Peebles, Sr., and she is Co-Pastor of the City of Praise Family Ministries in Landover, Maryland. Together, they are blessed to have four amazing and brilliant children – Joel, Jr., Janay, Jordan and Jeremiah. Ylawnda is a graduate of Bowie State University, where she graduated with high honors earning the Magna Cum Laude Award, she has her Master's Degree in Divinity from Wilbur Henry Waters School of Divinity, a Doctorate of Divinity from Rivers Bible Institute and a Doctorate in Humane Letters from Breakthrough Bible College.

In 2003 she founded Heart to Heart Literacy Program. This non-profit charitable organization was designed to inspire literacy in school aged children. She also wrote and published a children's book entitled, "God Loves Me Just the Way I Am", which is in its 3rd printing. She assists hundreds of women on their journey to health and wholeness through her efforts with her Transformation Squad, Kingdom Queen Organization, and the YP Rise Up Gratitude Journey, a live show on Facebook. Ylawnda co-hosts many ministry affairs such as the "Marry Me Again Experience" Marriage Events, "Touching the Hearts of People" telecast aired on the Impact Network, the Word of the Day aired on both Praise 104.1 and 105.1 WAVA stations in the Washington, DC Metropolitan Area.

Ylawnda was humbled and honored to receive the Coretta Scott King Award from the Prince George's Chapter of the Southern Christian Leadership Conference, the Catalyst of the Year Award from the Prince George's Chapter of Jack & Jill, Top Walk Team/Top Walker Fundraiser from NAMI Maryland, and Top Ten First Ladies from Praise 104.1.

Ylawnda is a member of the Alpha Kappa Alpha Sorority, Incorporated, and is faithfully committed to service for all mankind. She was grateful to receive, "New Soror of the Year in 2018.

"An empty life only focuses on personal achievement. True happiness is trusting in God, loving your family and making a substantial impact on one's community."

– Ylawnda Peebles